Uniforms of the Warsaw Pact

Published in the United States, 1978, by
Squadron/Signal Publications, Inc., 3461E. Ten Mile Road,
Warren, Michigan 48091.
Published in Great Britain, 1978, by
Arms and Armour Press, Lionel Leventhal Limited,
2-6 Hampstead High Street, London NW3 1QQ,
and at 4-12 Tattersalls Lane, Melbourne, Victoria 3000.

ISBN 0 85368 252 6

First German-language edition, published 1975,

Printed in Great Britain by
T. & A. Constable Ltd, Edinburgh

Uniforms of the Warsaw Pact

Friedrich Wiener

squadron/signal publications

Contents

Note: in many cases, East European army ranks have no direct equivalent in the armies of Britain or the United States. Readers will therefore find that literal translations have been used for such ranks in this book.

Introduction

For a very long time, the study of dress has failed to give due attention to the subject of army uniforms. This booklet seeks, at least in some degree, to rectify this with regard to the military dress of the Warsaw Pact countries.

The colour charts show uniform styles of the various armies: the black and white illustrations show the actual wearing of these uniforms, together with the variations that may occur from force to force.

The scope of the book has been extended by including insignia used on vehicles and aircraft of the East European armies.

The production of this work has been made possible chiefly by the efforts of Prof Dr Walter Hummelberger (Vienna), Dir Bernard Jamin (Strasbourg), Dr Nikolaus Krivinyi (Vienna), Robert Spiering (Hamburg) and Count Ernesto Vitetti (Romania). The colour charts have been provided by Ferenc Illes; the other sketches by Reserve Captain Franz Gruber.

Friedrich Wiener

Military Strengths of the Warsaw Pact Countries 1975

(plus Yugoslavia)

USSR

Strategic missile troops	350,000
Ground forces	1·82 million
Air force	400,000
Navy	500,000*
Trained Reserve	25 million

Bulgaria

Ground forces	123,000
Air force	22,000
Navy	10,000
Trained Reserve	285,000

German Democratic Republic

Ground forces	100,000
Air force	30,000
Navy	20,000
Trained Reserve	260,000

Poland

Ground forces	230,000
Air force	60,000
Navy	25,000
Trained Reserve	550,000

Romania

Ground forces	145,000
Air force	21,000
Navy	9,000
Trained Reserve	490,000

Czechoslovakia

Ground forces	160,000
Air force	50,000
Trained Reserve	350,000

Hungary

Ground forces	95,000
Air force	15,000
Trained Reserve	170,000

Yugoslavia

Ground forces	190,000
Air force	20,000
Navy	20,000
Trained Reserve	550,000

* Including 75,000 of the Naval Air Force, 17,000 Marines and 10,000 of the Coast Artillery Forces.

USSR

An ordinance of 26 July 1969 by the Russian Defence Ministry set out uniform changes which were to come into force on 1 January 1970 and be completed within two years. Field uniforms were also affected.
For all ranks there is always a distinction between summer and winter dress.
For non-commissioned officers and private soldiers serving for limited periods of time (conscripts), three uniforms are provided:

Field Uniform or Service Uniform ('Everyday Uniform');
Parade Uniform or Walking Out Uniform;
Work Dress.

For officers and long-service NCOs the following were laid down:

Field Uniform;
Service Uniform ('Everyday Uniform');
Parade/Walking Out Uniform and Parade/Service Uniform.

In the case of the Field Uniform, which is identical for officers, NCOs and men, the traditional Russian uniform shirt with an upright collar was replaced by a field blouse with a turn-down collar. Shoulder straps and collar patches are the same colour as the uniform material: buttons are in camouflage colour. With the field uniform, a steel helmet or a cap is worn: in winter a fur hat. A beret was introduced for airborne troops. The badges of the different branches of the service are in a dull material on the collar patches, with badges of rank on the shoulder straps.

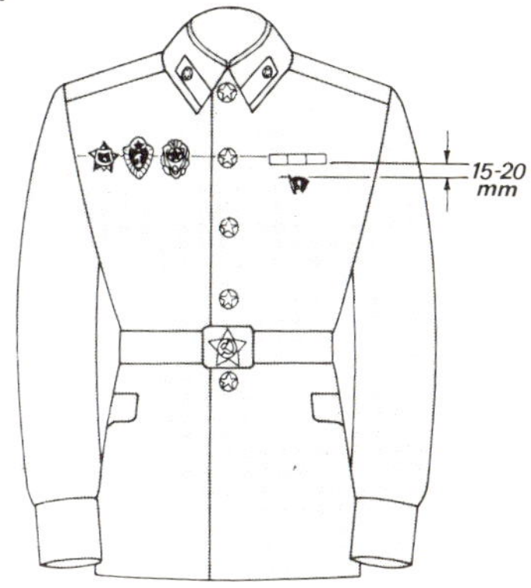

Field blouse of a Service Uniform ('Everyday Uniform') for conscripted NCOs and men, also showing how decorations are worn.

Red Army soldiers (left) with the East German People's Army (right) during an exercise. While the Soviet men have already been equipped with the new field uniforms, the lieutenant in the foreground is wearing the old-type uniform shirt. On his right breast the Guards' badge can be seen.

Gun crew on a 122mm M-38 medium field howitzer. Gunners do not carry packs, only water bottles, cartridge pouches and NBC protection masks. The AK-47 machine-carbine ('Kalashnikov') is invariably carried on the backs of those operating heavy weaponry.

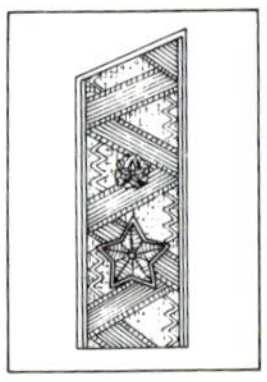

New badge of rank for Army Generals

Introduced 1974. Five-pointed star, 50mm across. Bears service branch insignia surrounded by a laurel wreath.

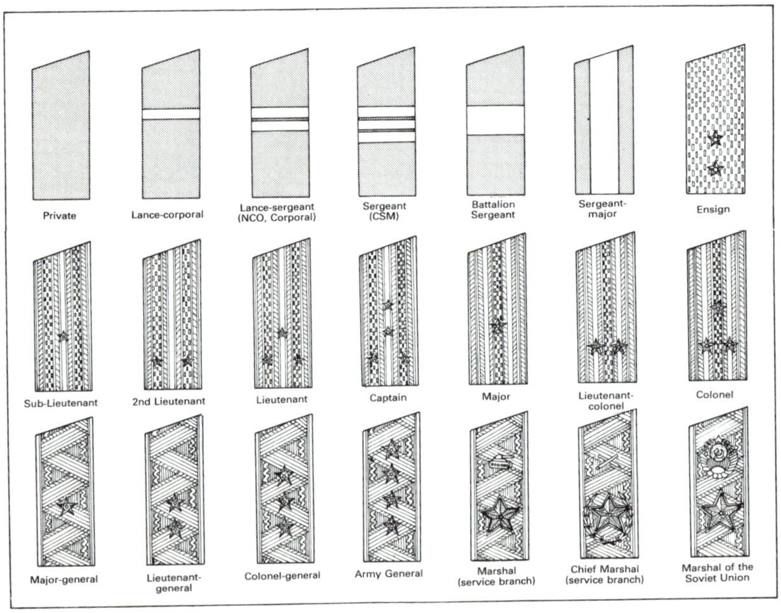

Soviet Army Badges of Rank

Officers of the various service branches (Armoured Corps, Artillery, Engineers, Signals, Flying Corps), after attaining the rank of Colonel-general, can become Marshal or Chief Marshal (e.g. Chief Marshal in the Armoured Corps). General Staff Officers go from Colonel-general to Army General and to Marshal of the Soviet Union. In the Service departments (Technical, Medical, Administration, etc.), the highest rank that can be reached is Colonel-general.

Armoured corps personnel wearing protective clothing: summer clothing bottom right; winter clothing bottom left.

Officer in winter uniform with fur hat and fur jacket (above). Soviet soldier in winter camouflage uniform, with a GT-T amphibious vehicle (left).

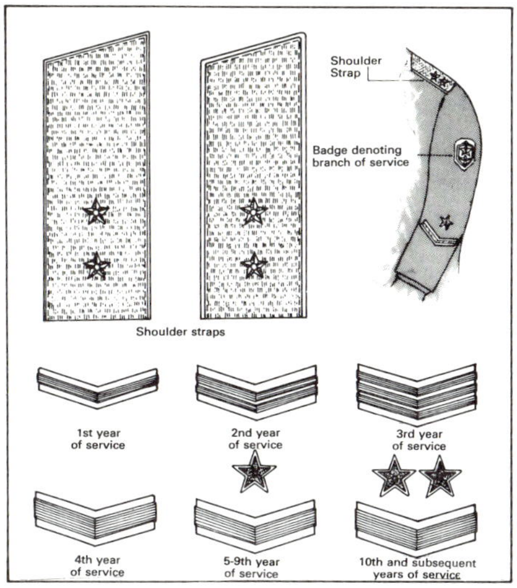

The rank of Ensign was introduced on 1 January 1972. This rank falls between officer and non-commissioned officer, and is awarded to long-serving NCOs: the idea being to take some of the load off lower rank officers in various units of the Red Army. On his Field Uniform, the Ensign wears only his badges of rank (on the shoulder straps). The appropriate long-service stripes are worn on Service and Walking Out Dress. Additionally, the Walking Out Dress carries any weapon proficiency badges to which the Ensign may be entitled.

Paratroops in Winter Dress, with fur hats and fur jackets.

March past of paratroops. They wear the Guards' badge and various proficiency badges.

Airborne troops with heavy weapons: an anti-tank gun crew (85mm M-45 with auxiliary propulsion): they wear berets (above): (below) a gun crew mans a 122mm M-63 gun howitzer: they wear parachuting hats.

Soldiers from an anti-aircraft rocket battery, distinguished by weapon-colour shoulder straps and collar patches. A captain is on the left; two lance-corporals are in the first file.

Members of an SPz crew in Battle Dress, with a lieutenant in the foreground. The gunlayer and driver are wearing armoured corps protective dress.

Border troops on patrol in Service Uniform. For service in the southern regions of the USSR in Asia, a lighter uniform with a hat was introduced.

An NBC defence group in protective clothing. The soldiers belong to an anti-aircraft rocket battery equipped with GANNEF type anti-aircraft rockets.

A two-man guard of the Border Troops, wearing Service Dress with overjacket in camouflage colours.

Soldiers from an anti-aircraft rocket battery, in winter uniform with fur hats.

Paratroops in winter uniform with fur hats and fur jackets. Jumping equipment is worn, in contrast to the picture on page 9. In the background stands an AN-12 (CUB) heavy transport plane, capable of carrying 100 fully armed paratroops.

Soviet Defence Minister, Marshal of the Soviet Union Andrej A. Gretschko and the Head of the Army and Fleet Political Directorate, Army General Alexei A. Jepischew inspect a unit of the Soviet Marine Infantry.

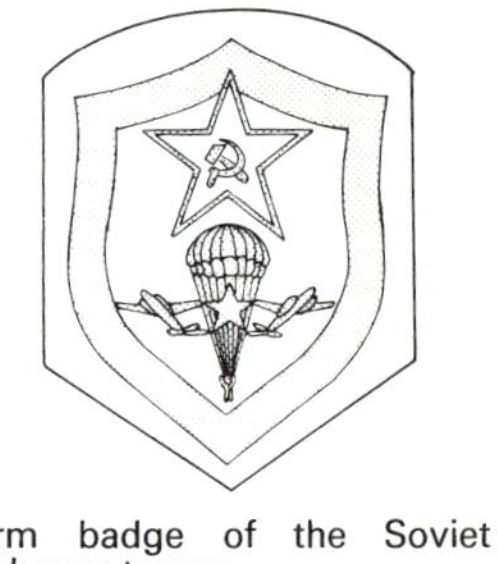

Arm badge of the Soviet airborne troops.

Members of a Marine Infantry unit manning a BTR-60P armoured personnel carrier; their weapon is a 7·62mm machine-gun PKS ('Kalashnikov'). The soldiers are wearing overjackets in camouflage colours.

Pilots in special clothing (below) and in leather jackets (below right).

The field uniforms of the USSR, like their equipment, are simple and practical. They reflect the idea of the soldier as held by the Russian people. They do not have Battle Dress as we know it. Occasionally, special units such as airborne troops and marine infantry wear overjackets in camouflage colours. More recently, coarse mesh net appeared on steel helmets.

In the case of short-service NCOs and men, the Field Uniform and Service Uniform ('Everyday Uniform') are one and the same. In the case of long-service soldiers, shoulder straps and collar patches are in a 'weapon' colour. The airborne troops wear a light-blue beret and a branch of service badge on the left upper arm.

Bulgaria

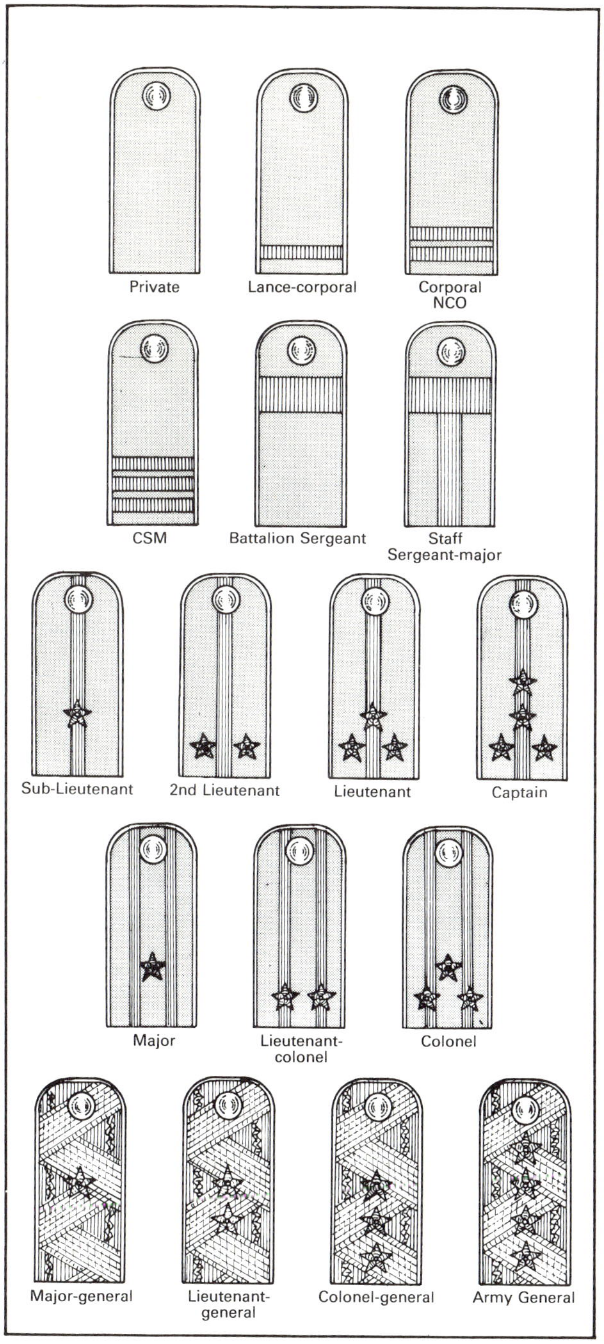

Badges of rank of the Bulgarian People's Army

Above: Soldier from a Bulgarian motorized rifle unit which is equipped with armoured cars. He is armed with an AK-47 machine-carbine ('Kalashnikov') and with the protective headgear issued to tank crews.

Below: Two Bulgarian paratroopers with jumping equipment: they carry the Soviet machine-carbine AK-47 ('Kalashnikov') with folding (collapsible) metal butt.

The present uniform of the Bulgarian People's Army dates back essentially to 1936. Relatively small changes — affecting chiefly insignia and badges — were made later. Russian Army uniforms long provided a pattern followed by the Bulgarians. On 29 December 1970, the Bulgarian War Ministry authorized the introduction of new Field Service and Walking Out Uniforms. This was done in stages with the Walking Out Uniform issued first. The new Field Uniforms are being issued to only a few units on a trial basis. In view of Bulgaria's economic difficulties, it seems likely that full re-equipping will take a long time.

Above: Bulgarian Air Force pilots in Flying Service Dress.

Above right: Motorized troops manning a 14·5mm KPV quadruply mounted anti-aircraft machine-gun. ZPU-4.

Badges

Field Cap Peaked Cap

Below: Soldiers of the Bulgarian People's Army camping in winter conditions.

Mountain troops in winter equipment with snow camouflage.

Men of the Bulgarian War Fleet in Sea-going Service Dress; left: a sailor with radio equipment; right: an NCO at a weapon-control point.

Officer's Preparatory School personnel (cadets) of the Bulgarian People's Army in Service Dress.

Motorized troops of the Bulgarian People's Army, in winter Battle Dress with overcoats. They are armed with Soviet machine-carbine AK-47 ('Kalashnikov'): in the centre is an anti-tank gunner with an RPG-7.

Commander and driver as permanent crew of an armoured personnel carrier BTR-60PB, in protective clothing as worn by tank crews (summer version).

Wireless operator of a motorized rifle regiment, in winter Battle Dress with an overcoat and steel helmet.

Three men of a tank crew in protective clothing (winter version).

German Democratic Republic

For its land, air and border forces, the East German National People's Army (NVA) uses the following uniforms: Field Service Uniform (Battle Dress) summer and winter, Service Uniform, Staff Service Uniform both for parade and walking out; additionally, there is special clothing for armoured corps troops (protective clothing) and for paratroops. The Staff Service Uniform is only worn by officers and full-time NCOs. It may also be worn for walking out. Soldiers and NCOs (corporals) undergoing basic training use the Parade Uniform for walking out. Conscripts may, at their own expense, acquire a two-piece plain Walking Out Uniform made of the same material as the Staff Service Uniform. Equipment consists usually of: steel helmet, belt and leather belt, carrying frame, assault kit (parts I and II), water bottle, mess tins, ground sheets with accessories, and a wool blanket.

The three illustrations on this page show motorized troops of the National People's Army in summer Battle Dress.

Gunlayer in summer Battle Dress using an anti-tank gun: his steel helmet has a camouflage covering.

Ceremonial handing-over of weapons to recruits. A Party functionary hands a young soldier a machine-carbine MPiKM (AK-47 'Kalashnikov').

NCO (corporal) in summer Battle Dress: steel helmet has a camouflage net.

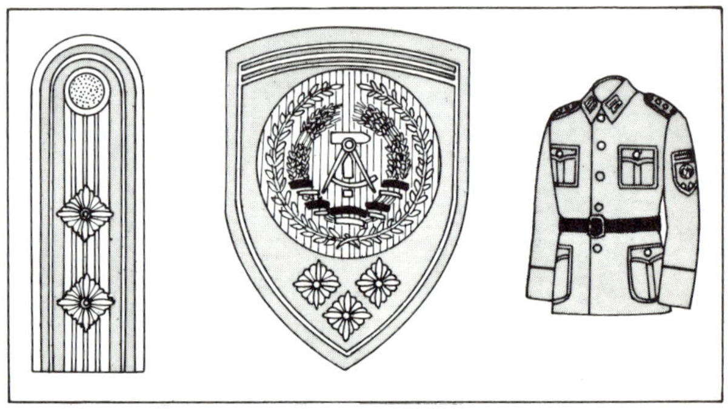

An Ensign's insignia, worn on the left upper sleeve of the field jacket and overcoat (centre). From their eleventh year of service, ensigns wear one star: from their sixteenth year, two stars and from their twenty-first, three stars. A shoulder strap of the Battle Dress is shown (left) and the way of wearing these is shown on the right.

The rank of Ensign on the Soviet pattern was introduced into the NVA on 13 December 1973. It is mandatory for an NCO (sergeant) to have passed an Ensign's course. This measure is to ensure that older and more experienced NCOs stay longer with their units. In most service particulars — for example those of uniform — the ensign is equivalent to an officer.

Service rank insignia of the East German National People's Army

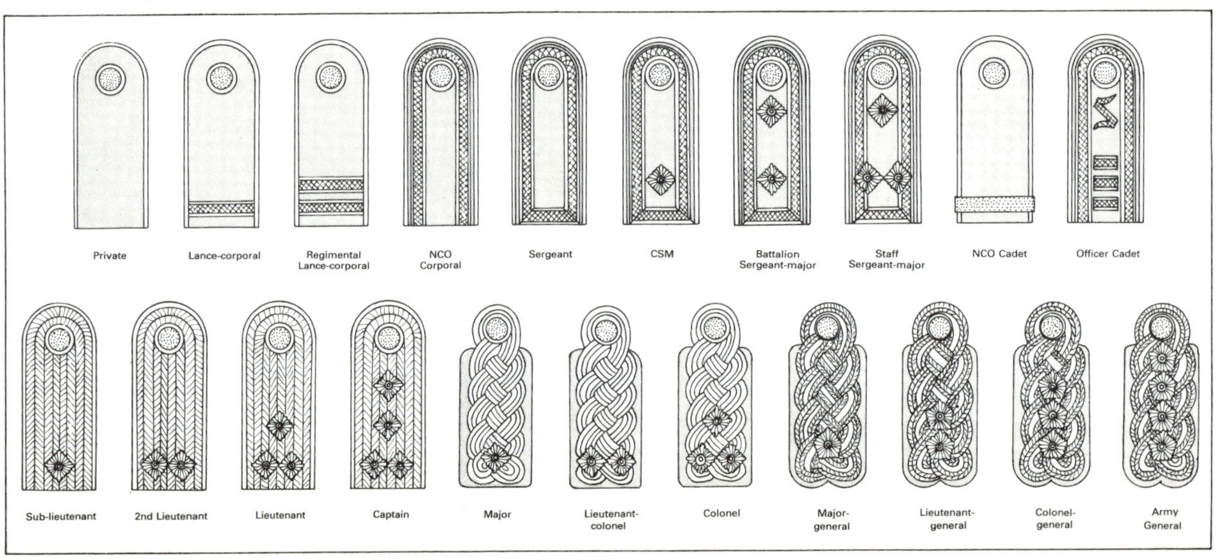

Paratrooper in summer Battle Dress with grey-brown beret. On parade, a bright red(!) beret is worn. For jumping, a protective cap is worn under the jumping helmet.

Sentry at a training ground, in summer Battle Dress.

Right: tank crew member with the new-type protective headwear. Usually, however, the old-type Soviet protective headwear is worn.

Below: paratroops of the NVA, with jumping equipment.

Wireless operator of an NVA unit, in an older type Battle Dress of camouflage pattern. The soldier seen in the illustration is a Reservist.

Service rank insignia of the 'Workers Combat Teams' — official nomenclature — 'Appointment insignia of the Combat Soldiers' — worn on jumping, right upper sleeve.

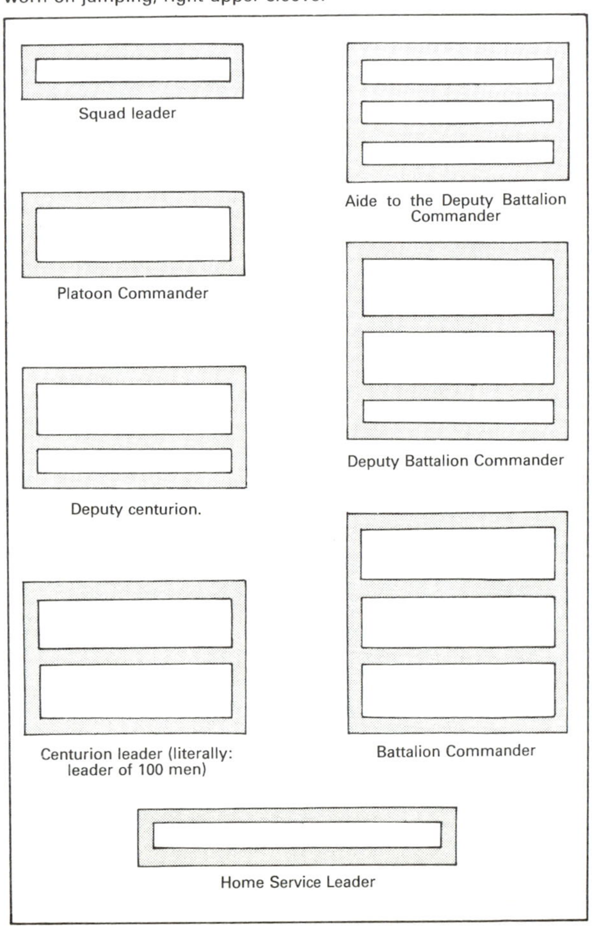

Gun crew in summer Battle Dress.

A patrol of the NVA Border Guards in summer Service Dress.

Members of the 'Workers Combat Teams' undergoing weapon training on a Soviet recoilless 82mm B10 anti-tank gun. The 'Battlers' are equipped with machine-carbine AK-47 ('Kalashnikov'), and wear insignia of their battle group on the left upper sleeve.

Poland

Recruits being attested

The Colour Party wear Parade Dress; the four recruits are wearing Service Uniform, which is very much the same as Battle Dress. National symbolism plays a more significant role in the Polish Army than in the other Warsaw Pact countries. In this picture, the Polish Eagle adorns the tip of the flag-pole. The saluting podium is similarly adorned with it.

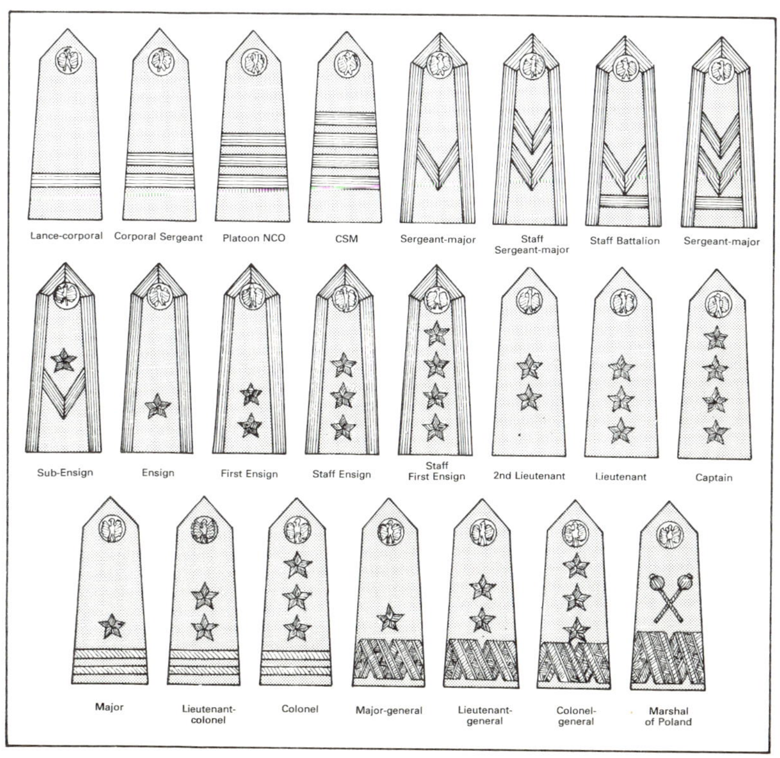

Service rank insignia

In the case of NCOs and men, the service ranks correspond to some extent with the similar ranks in the Austrian, Swiss and German (Federal Republic) armies. Paratroop officers wear their badges of rank also on their berets.

Left to right. A Polish paratrooper; a soldier of the Soviet Army, a soldier from the Czechoslovak People's Army and a soldier from the East German People's Army.

This illustration is typical of Soviet Military Propaganda ('Brothers in Arms'). It appeared in the East German publication *Militärtechnik* ('Military Technology') together with a quotation from Lenin: 'Capitalism is an international force: to combat it we need an international association of the workers: an international alliance.'

Right: A soldier in summer Battle Dress, wearing the headgear of a tank crewman, hands down the theodolite of an armed rocket-launcher T-7A 'SCUD-A'.

Below: Polish Army engineers building a PMP bridge during manoeuvres. These manoeuvres entitled 'Schild 72' (Shield 72) (see also Truppendienst (lit. Army Service) from Volume 1/1973 pages 20 to 24): The soldiers are in summer Battle Dress. The engineer on the left has a lifejacket fitting over his 'Kalashnikov' AK-47 machine-carbine.

Soldiers from a Polish rocket-launching unit with heavy rocket-launchers FROG-4 (top left and below) and a similar SCUD-A (top right). The crews are wearing different kinds of protective clothing. In the lower picture, with back to the camera, is an officer in a Service Uniform who is in charge of the training operation.

Romania

Romanian Army officers discussing field tactics.

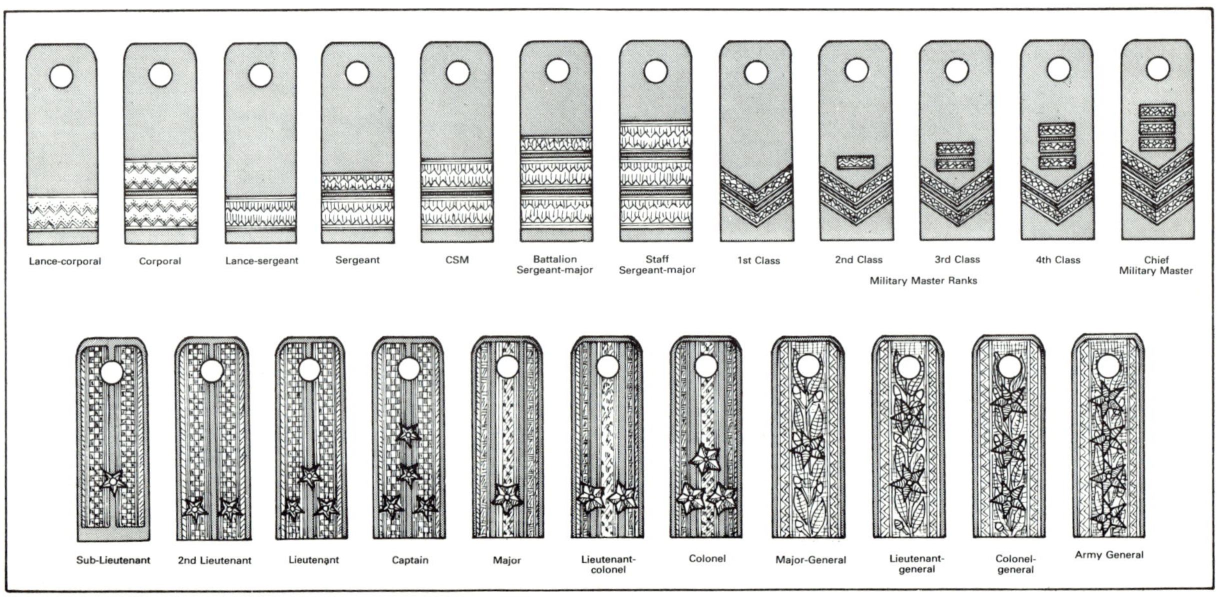

Service rank insignia of reserve officers have, at their outer edges, a piping in basic (weapon) colours. (See, for example, the Sub-Lieutenant).

Motorized troops leaving Soviet type BTR-60PB armoured personnel carrier. In the foreground is a machine-gunner carrying a light machine-gun 7·62mm RPK ('Kalashnikov'). The other three soliders' camouflage suits are worn generally by border troops, but only by certain Army units.

An Officer of the motorized troops with his wireless operator.

A motorized rifleman throwing a hand-grenade.

Above: solidiers at the Artillery School in Service Dress — in essentials this is similar to the Field Uniform. The men are undergoing practical training.

Below: members of the 'Patriotic Guard' with submachine-guns during tactical training. The object of the exercise is the defence of installations against 'Attack by Enemy Terrorists'.

Armoured Corps troops, in protective clothing, on a Soviet armoured personnel carrier BTR-50PU (Command and Radio Vehicle).

Launching preparations for an anti-aircraft rocket of Soviet Type M-2 (GUIDELINE). The crew are wearing Work Dress.

Right: the Romanian Defence Minister, Colonel-general Ion Ionita reviews a detachment of mountain troops. He is travelling in a 5-ton (4×4) ARO M-461-C lorry (built under licence in Romania on the Soviet pattern 5-ton GAS-69A).

Below: march past of a unit of the 'Patriotic Guards'. It is equipped with AK-47 ('Kalashnikov') machine-carbines. Most of the 'Patriotic Guards' are still equipped with older weapons.

Both photographs were taken at a Romanian National Holiday Parade which takes place yearly on 23 August in Bucharest.

Above: 'Patriotic Guards' — Intermediate Pupils (from an Upper School) undergoing military training in the field.

Pilots from an MiG-21 squadron in flying Service Dress.

Right: officer candidates of the Romanian Navy being instructed in the use of navigational equipment. A Lieutenant Commander (lit. Lieutenant Captain) is their instructor. The photograph was taken at the Naval Academy at Konstanza.

Below: sailors of the Romanian Navy at a national Holiday parade in Bucharest. They are armed with AK-47 ('Kalashnikov') 7·62mm machine-carbines.

Czechoslovakia

The present uniforms of the Czech People's Army (CVA) were introduced in 1964–65. Until then, soldiers of the CVA wore olive-green uniforms corresponding, in cut, largely to the Soviet pattern. In 1964, the CVA reverted to a khaki colour, and to the style of the Czech pre-war uniform.

Service and Walking Out Uniforms are identical in cut and colour. Other ranks wear bronze coloured metal buttons on the field blouse of the Walking Out Uniform: NCOs wear silver buttons, officers wear golden ones. The Service Uniform has buttons of grey material. With the Walking Out Uniform, a light-coloured shirt is worn with a brown tie, and also long trousers and brown shoes. With the Service Uniform goes an olive-coloured shirt with a tie of a similar hue. For summer wear, an olive-coloured shirt-blouse was introduced. According to the branch of service, the long trousers of the Service Dress are replaced by lace-up half-length boots with tucked-in trousers. Both kinds of dress are accompanied by a flat cap.

The Sleeve Insignia of the Flying Units is carried on the left upper sleeve in Service and Walking Out uniforms.

The various branches of the Army are distinguished by insignia worn on the collar of the field blouse. Border Troops have green collar patches bearing the traditional dog's head. Additionally, the caps worn by border troops have a green covering.

In the mid-1960s a new Battle Dress was introduced. 'Earthworm' camouflage replaced the conventional large-pattern camouflage. The side parts of the Field Cap could be turned down. Above the half-length lace-up boots, tucked-in trousers with overhang were worn. There were no branch of service differentiating insignia on the Battle Dress.

With the uniform changes of 1965, new service rank insignia were introduced. The form of these was influenced by that of the first Czech Republic. On the officers' shoulder patches were crossed maces reminiscent of those of Hussite times (Palcat).

On the Battle Dress, the badges of rank are on the right breast. The rectangular badge is 9cm by 5·5cm in size.

Motorized troops in overcoats or winter Battle Dress with a Soviet 82mm B-10 recoilless anti-tank gun.

Right: motorized troops in summer Battle Dress, armed with M-58 machine-carbines.

Left: vehicle sign of traffic controllers of the Traffic Control Units.
(N.B. 'P' is equivalent to 'R' in the cyrillic alphabet, and 'R' is the initial letter of the German term 'Regulierer').

Below: a traffic control unit in their 5-ton GAS-69 lorry. On the bonnet is their vehicle sign and on the door is the Czech National insignia.

Motorized troops of the Czech People's Army dismount from an OT-64 'SKOT' armoured personnel carrier. The soldiers are equipped with M-58 machine-carbines, the Czech version of the Soviet AK-47 'Kalashnikov' machine-carbine. The vehicle crew, commandant and driver as well as gunner and loader in the turret, wear the protective clothing for armoured troops.

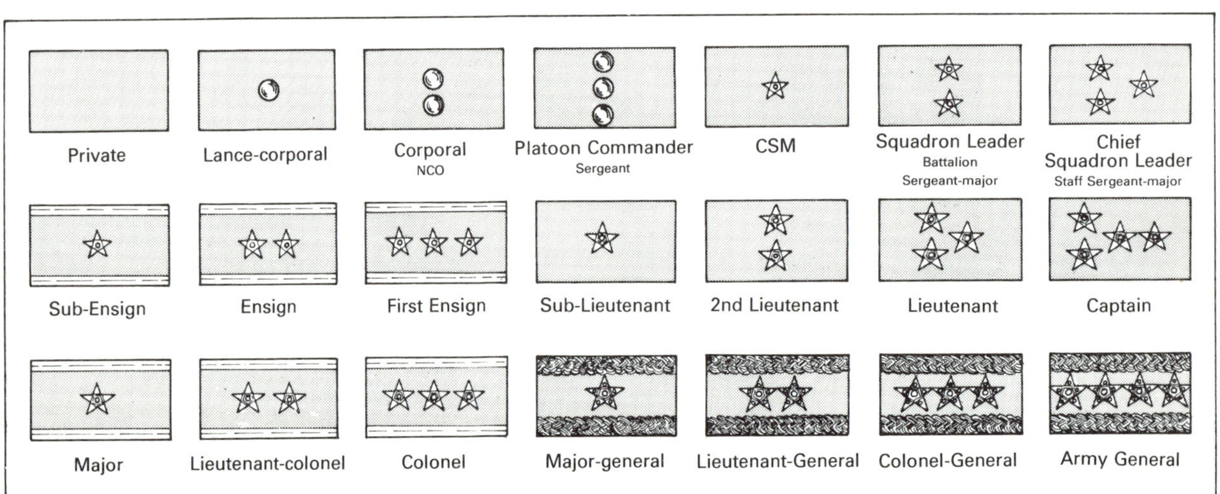

Service Rank Insignia on the Battle Dress

The stars and braid worn by NCOs, like those of Ensigns, are light-grey. The stars of Officers and braid of Staff Officers are yellow. Generals have reddish-brown plaited braid with their yellow stars.

A nationality badge of the CVA, used on vehicles and shown on both sides.

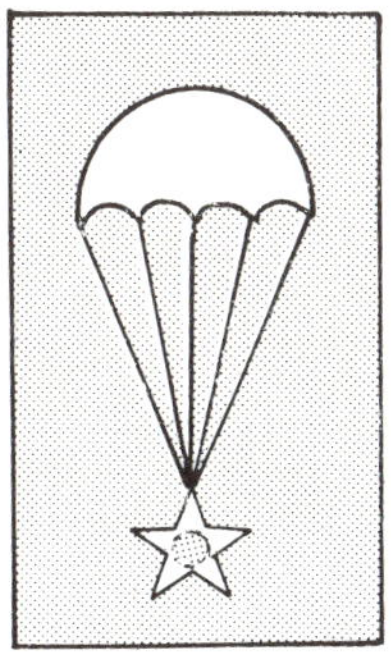

Vehicle badge for airborne troops.

Above: gun crew on a 122mm M-38 medium field howitzer, in summer Battle Dress and field caps. They are equipped with M-58 machine-carbines, but carry only ammunition pouches and containers for an NBC protective mask.

Left: a squad leader (Sergeant) of paratroops in old-style Battle Dress. This was used until 1965, although it was by no means in complete general issue. It is now rare. However, in the event of mobilization it could well be issued again.

Armoured Corps troops in their protective clothing. Weapon is an M-58 machine-carbine.

Above: vehicle badge of border troops. This is carried on both sides of the vehicle, with the dog's head always pointing in the direction of travel.

Left: a soldier of the border Troops in Service Dress. His weapon is an AK-47 machine-carbine ('Kalashnikov').

Above: a soldier of the Danube Border patrol, in summer Service Dress, stationed on the Danube at Pressburg.
Border troops have green coverings on their protective caps and sailor caps.

Left: soldiers of the Danube Border Guard at a parade in Prague. They are armed with self-loading carbines M-52/57.

Members of the People's Militia (Territorial Defence) marching through Prague. They are armed with M-58 machine-carbines. The letters 'LM' on the armband signify 'Lidova Milice' (People's Militia).
A uniform change was introduced for the People's Militia on 1 January 1970. Principally, the armband was replaced by an arm badge. This had blue letters 'LM' on a red ground. Furthermore, they received the same Battle Dress as the army. In view of the well-known material shortages of Eastern bloc countries, it will take many years for this change to be fully implemented.

A patrol of the Czech-East German border: three soldiers from the Border Troops and a member of the People's Militia.

Bottom: a mixed squad of People's Militia men and Border Troops, on the march during an exercise, entering the Budweis district of South Bohemia.

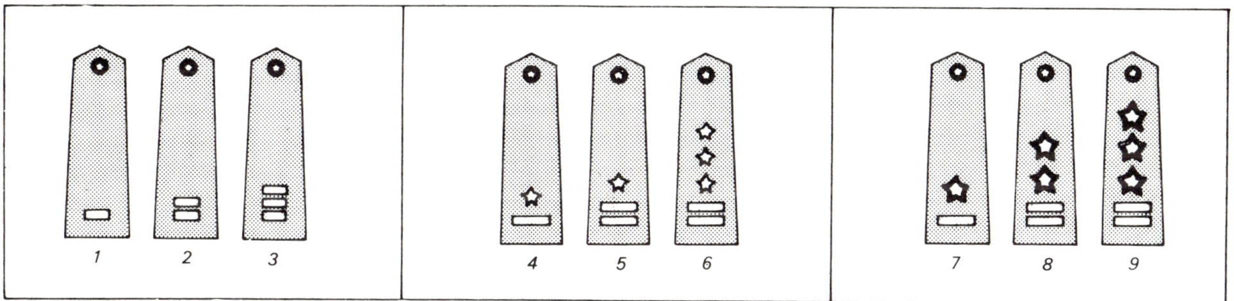

People's Militia Service Rank Insignia

Red Bars: 1 — Section Leader, 2 — Deputy Platoon Leader, 3 — Company Commander.
Gold Bars: 1 — Battalion Staff, 2 — Deputy Battalion Commander, 3 — Battalion Commander.

Silver Bars and Red Stars: 4 — District Detachment Staff, two stars — Deputy Commander of a District Detachment, three stars — Commander of a District Detachment; 5 — Staff of a Regional Detachment, two stars — Deputy Commander of a Regional Detachment; 6 — Commander of a Regional Detachment.

Gold Bars and larger Red Stars: 7 — People's Militia Staff in the Czech or Slovak Socialist Republic, two stars — Deputy Commander of a territory; three stars — Commander of a Territory; 8 — Chief of Staff of the People's Militia, with one star only — main Staff of the People's Militia; 9 — Commander of the People's militia in the CSSR.

Above: Air Force captain in flying Service Dress.

Left: soldiers of an anti-aircraft rocket battery, in working dress.

Below: Motorized troops boarding a transport helicopter of the Czech People's Army. This type of Soviet MI-8 (HIP) helicopter can carry up to 28 men.

Hungary

A section of a motorized rifle company of the Hungarian people's Army. The eight-man crew are travelling on a T-54 tank; their armament consists of six machine-carbines AK-47 ('Kalashnikov' — Hungarian version), a light machine-gun RPD and an RPG-2 anti-tank rocket projector.

Hungarian motorized troops in summer Battle Dress, crossing an obstacle by means of a TMM bridge.

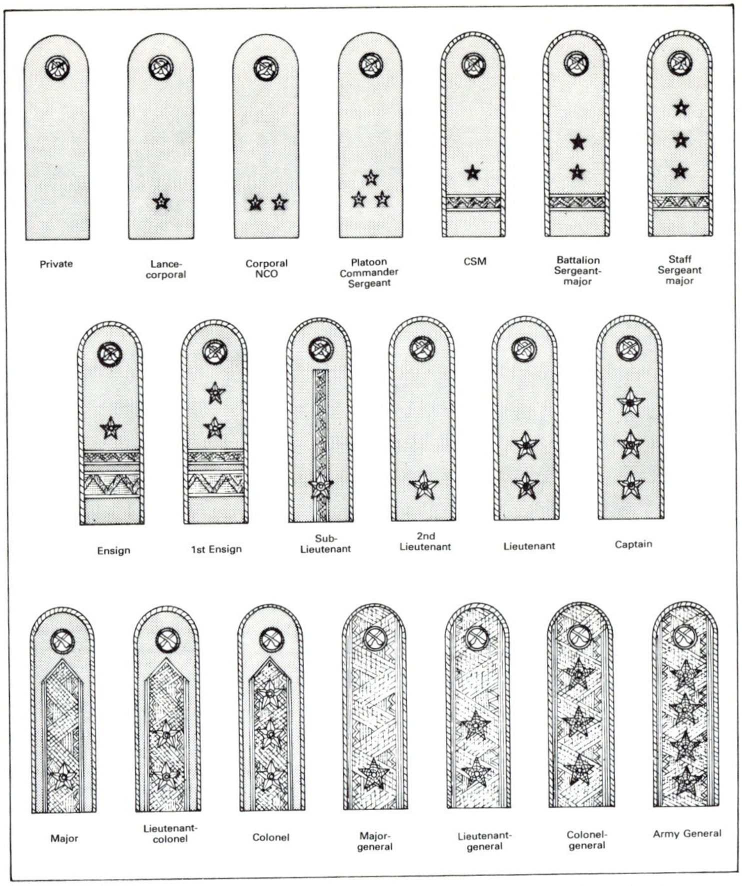

Service rank insignia of the Hungarian People's Army. Although there has been no Army General in Hungary for some years, the rank has been retained. Currently, an officer's career ends at Colonel-general. At the present time, the only Colonel-general is the Hungarian Defence minister, Lajos Czinege.

Arm badge of the Hungarian People's Army ('MN' = Magyar Nèphadsereg — Hungarian People's Army).

Arm badge of the Hungarian Border Troops ('HÖR = Hàtarör — Border Guard). This and the preceding badge are worn on the left upper arm of the Service and Walking Out uniforms, and also on the windcheater (anorak).

Left: soldiers of a Hungarian Armoured Reconnaissance Unit with a recoilless anti-tank gun (rPaK) 107mm B-11. This gun crew wear protective dress for tank crews, with the battle pack as worn by motorized troops. In the background is a Hungarian FUG armoured reconnaissance vehicle.

Three soldiers from an Armoured Reconnaissance unit in Battle Dress with Field Caps.

Hungarian motorized troops in winter Battle Dress, manhandling a 107mm B-11 recoilless anti-tank gun into place.

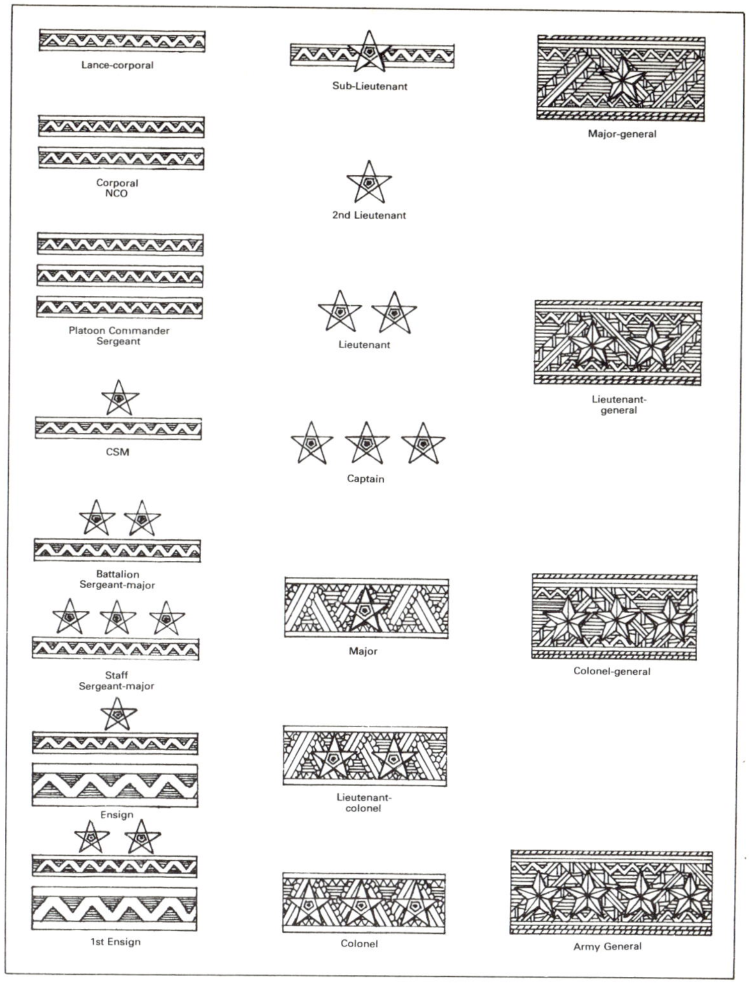

Service rank insignia of the Hungarian People's Army, worn on the left side of the Field Cap. The colour is brown.

Below: during a battle exercise, the Medical Corps of the Hungarian People's Army carry off a 'wounded' man. The soldiers are wearing summer Battle Dress. The ambulance is an East German 2-ton (4×4) 'Robur' LO-1800. In the background is a 2-ton 'Robur' 30K.

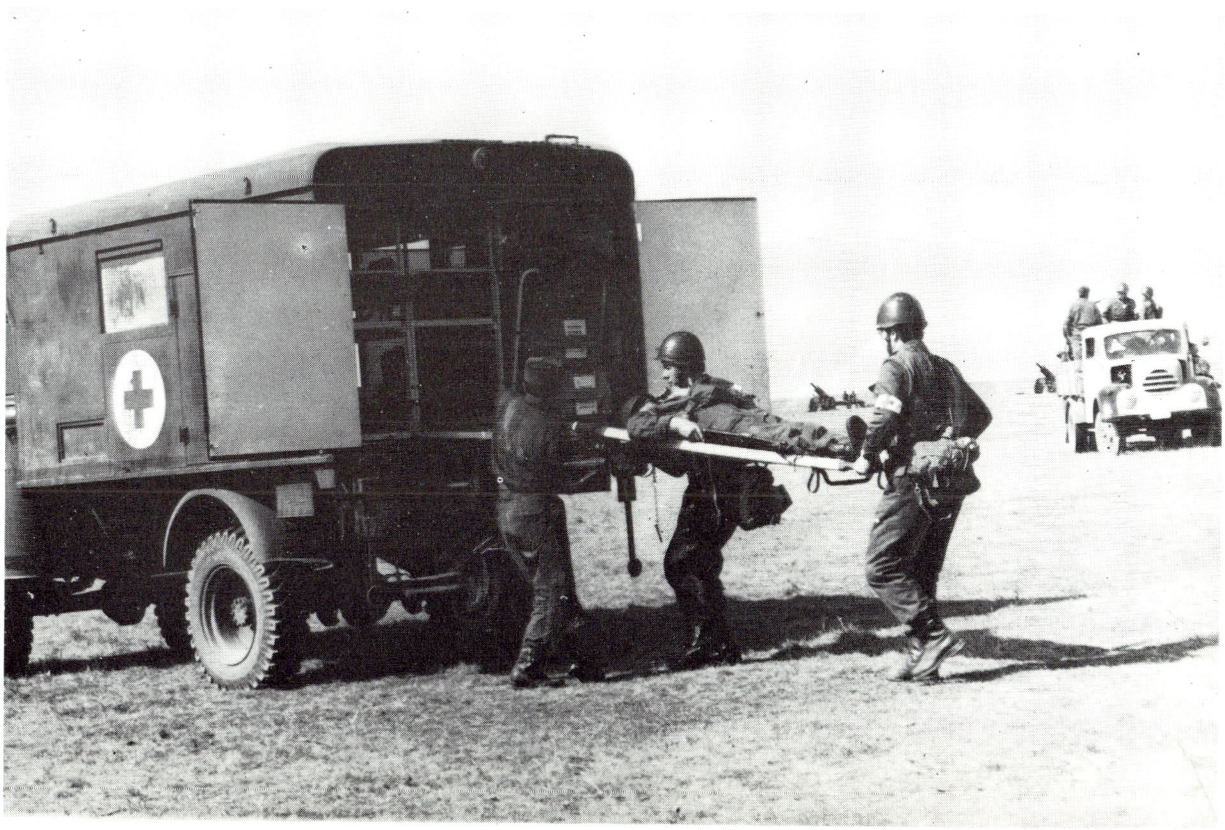

Above: a unit of the Hungarian Workers' Militia at a march past in Budapest (1 May 1973).

Left: a higher-rank leader of the Workers' Militia makes a symbolic handing-over of a Soviet sub-machine-gun M-41 (PPSH) to members of a Communist Youth formation.

Below: a member of the Hungarian Workers' Militia standing Guard of Honour at the Parliament building in Bucharest. The armband of the Workers' Militia can be clearly seen; it is only worn on the shirt however.

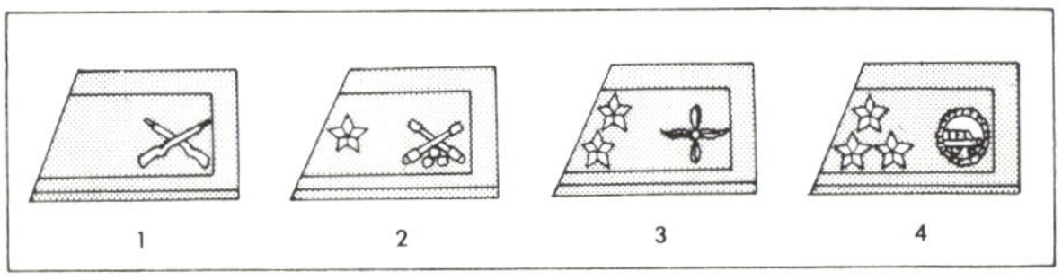

Service rank insignia of Service and Walking Out Uniforms
1 — Private (Motorized troops); 2 — Lance-corporal (Artillery); 3 — Corporal (Air force); 4 — Platoon Commander (Army Service Corps). The arrangement of stars is identical with that used in the Austro-Hungarian Army up to 1918.

Shared guard duty. A patrol consisting of two soldiers of the Hungarian People's Army and a member of the Workers' Militia reporting to the Duty Officer. The soldiers wear summer Battle Dress with Field Caps. The officer is wearing Service/Walking Out Uniform.

Yugoslavia

Above: soldiers from an anti-tank platoon with an 82mm M-60 recoilless anti-tank gun.

Right: a Sergeant-major (of Cavalry)—his badge of rank may be seen on the left breast — hands a corporal a commomorative badge for the manoeuvre 'Freiheit 71' ('Freedom 71') (in Yugoslav 'Sloboda 71') in Croatia, October 1971. The soldiers are already equipped with the new Field Cap which is to be introduced into all units of the Yugoslav People's Army.

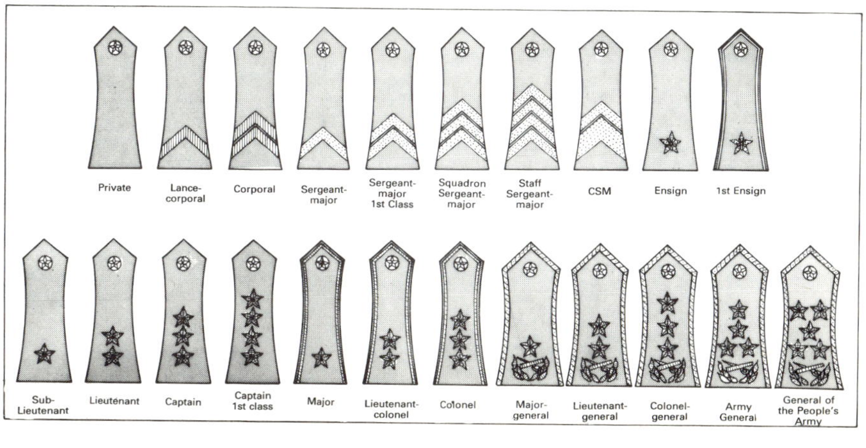

Service badges of rank of the Yugoslav People's Army, which are worn on the shoulder boards of Field, Service and Walking Out uniforms.
The rank of 'Oberleutnant' (lieutenant) is expressed colloquially in the Army as 'Leutnant' (2nd Lieutenant). The method of addressing him is 'Comrade 2nd Lieutenant'.

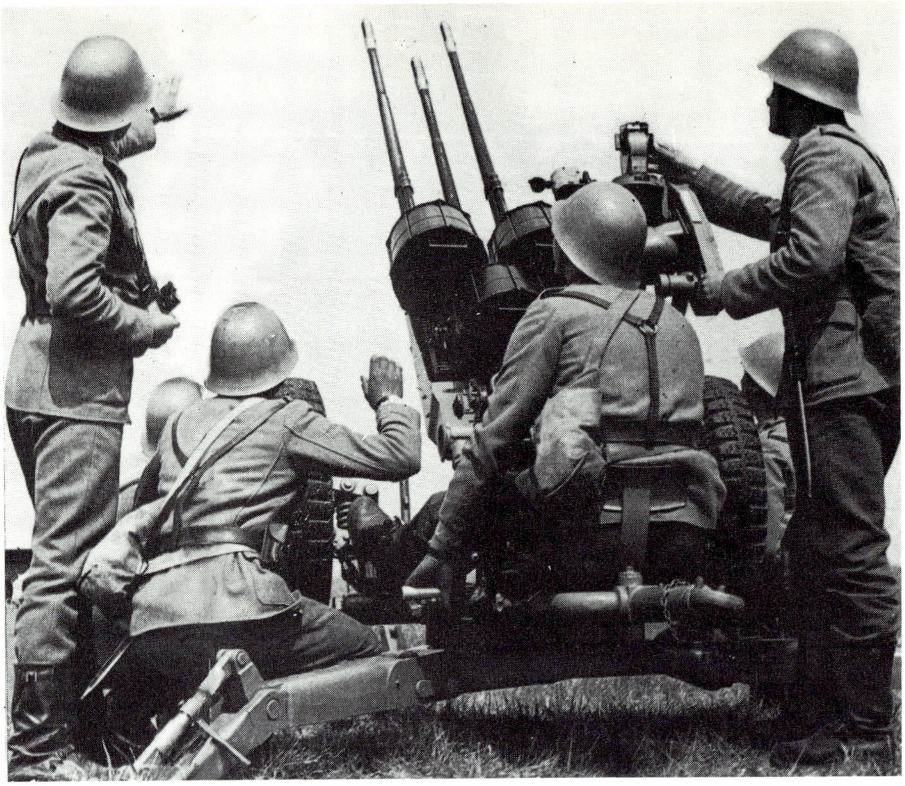

Above: the crew of a 20mm M-57 (3-barrelled anti-aircraft cannon).
Below: a heavy mortar 120mm UBM-52 being brought into position.

The uniforms of the Yugoslav People's Army are simple and practical, and have been so for many years.
In the case of other ranks, many articles of the Field Uniform are similar to those of the Service Uniform and Walking Out Uniform.
A uniform modification has been in progress since 1971. The fore-and-aft cap of the Field Uniform is being replaced by a Field Cap with a peak similar to those already worn by the mountain troops. Lace-up boots with short leather gaiters are to replace existing boots.
The Territorial Militia, for whom the various provinces of the republic are responsible, is not as uniformly clad and equipped as the Yugoslav People's Army. Efforts are being made to achieve a parity, in this respect, with the Army.
The title 'Marshal' is used only for the President of the country, Josip Broz-Tito.

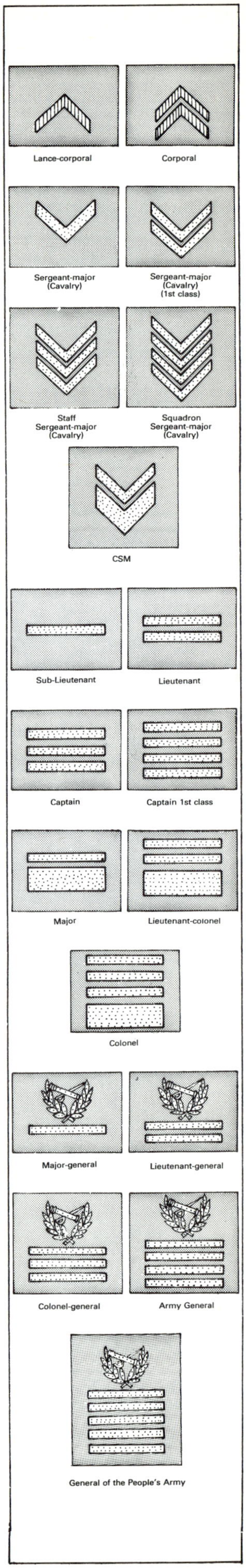

Right: Rank insignia as worn on raincoats, anoraks and miscellaneous items of clothing. Insignia is worn on the left breast-side.

1

2

1 — Members of the Territorial Militia in the older uniform.

2 — Members of the Territorial Militia in newer uniform (Field Cap).

3 — Pilot in Flying Service Uniform, with an American fighter-bomber (Thunderjet).

4 — Soldiers from a Signals unit, wearing groundsheets as rain-capes.

3

4

Medical Corps personnel take away a wounded man.

Mountain troops in winter equipment leaving an igloo.

The principal difference between the uniform of the Yugoslav Mountain Troops and that of the rest of the Army is their breeches, long stockings and climbing boots. The mountain cap is to be introduced throughout the People's Army.

Vehicle and Aircraft Insignia

Heavy field rocket-launchers FROG-7 of the Soviet Army. On the front vehicle is a nationality badge; there is none on the one in the background.

A rocket-launcher BM-21 on a lorry URAL-375D with the insignia of the Soviet Army Group in Germany ('CA' = 'SA' — Soviet Army).

A heavy field rocket-launcher FROG-4 of the Soviet Army on its travel-mounting on reconnaissance tank PT-76, the side wall of which bears the nationality insignia.

While aircraft insignia tend to be uniform, the nationality insignia of tanks and vehicles show considerable variation. Frequently the red star is missing from Soviet tanks and armoured vehicles.

A T-55 tank of a Soviet Army Guards Armoured Unit. The turret shows the Guards' insignia. (East Berlin, 8 May 1965).

1

2

3

4

1 A T-54 tank of the Hungarian People's Army (Budweis, 25 September 1966).

2 A Soviet URAL-375D lorry of the East German National People's Army, towing a field howitzer 122mm M-38 (Budweis, 25 September 1966).

3 Armoured car OT-64 SKOT of the Polish People's Army (Prague, 16 September 1972).

4 T-55 tank of the Polish People's Army (Exercise 'Schild 72' — September 1972).

Up to about 1967, Polish tanks carried, as national marking, the white Polish eagle.

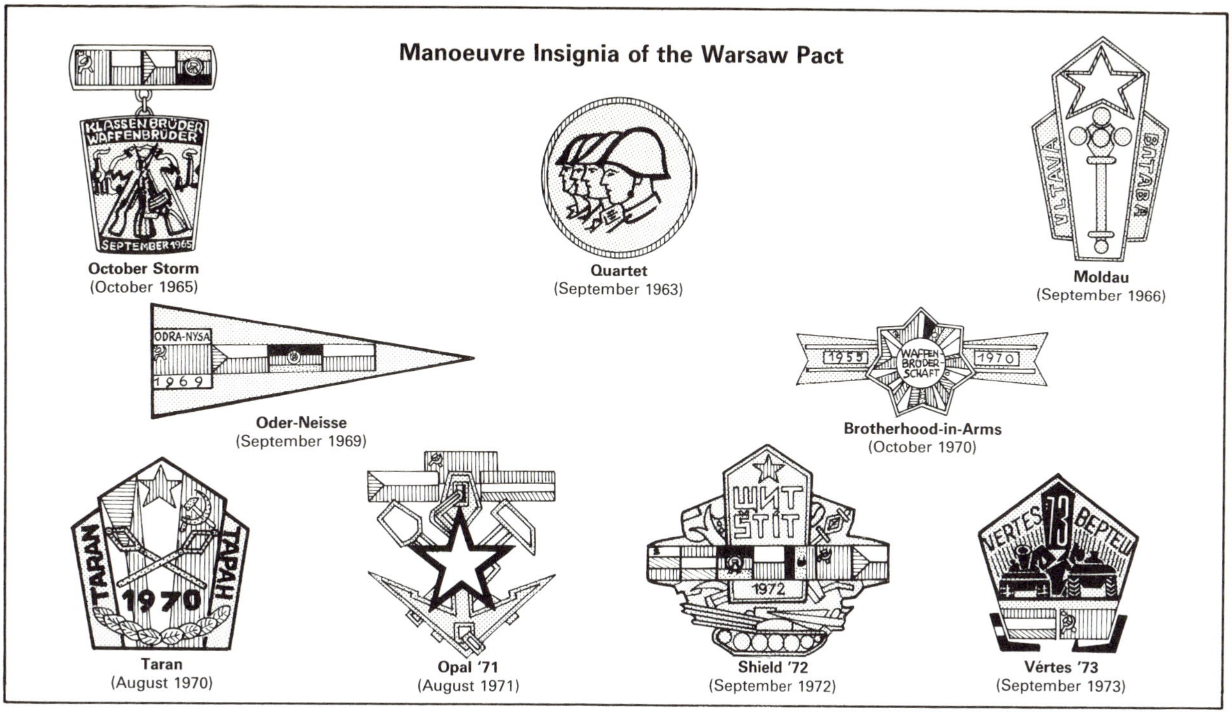

Manoeuvre Insignia of the Warsaw Pact

October Storm (October 1965)

Quartet (September 1963)

Moldau (September 1966)

Oder-Neisse (September 1969)

Brotherhood-in-Arms (October 1970)

Taran (August 1970)

Opal '71 (August 1971)

Shield '72 (September 1972)

Vértes '73 (September 1973)

After large Warsaw Pact manoeuvres, it is customary to give out commemorative badges. These may be worn on the uniform.

Decontaminating a 1·5-ton (4×4) Tatra 805 lorry of the Czechoslovak People's Army; the insignia is on the door of the cab.

Soviet heavy rocket-launchers FROG-7 of the Romanian Army. The nationality insignia is painted above the registration number. (Bucharest, 23 August 1971).

Above: Soviet all-weather fighter MiG-21PF (FISHBED-E).

The aircraft of front-line units of the tactical air arm of the Soviet Union, and combat aircraft of the various smaller Warsaw Pact countries have, for some time past, been painted in camouflage colours.

Left: tail unit showing the national marking of a Soviet transport aircraft AN-12 (CUB). An airborne tank, ASU-85 is being loaded into the aircraft; the insignia of the Soviet airborne arm is displayed on the side of the tank.

Below: training aircraft G-2A 'Galeb' of the Yugoslav People's Army.

Soviet fighter-trainer MiG-21UTI of the East German National People's Army.

Czech Training Aircraft Aero L-29 'Delfin' (MAYA).

A Bulgarian pilot climbing out of a trainer; on the tail unit of the aircraft behind his can be seen national markings differing slightly from the normal.

A Soviet transport helicopter Mi-4 (HOUND) of the East German People's Army; the national marking is comparatively large.

An OT-64 SKOT armoured personnel carrier of the Czechoslovak People's Army, with national marking and insignia of the airborne arm.

Above: A BTR-60P armoured personnel carrier with Soviet Marine-Infantry insignia on the bow plate and on the side armour.

Left: airborne tank ASU-85 bearing the Soviet airborne unit sign.

Below: Soviet airborne tank with Polish Airborne Troops insignia (Erfurt, 24 Oct 1965).

Lance-corporal of motorized troops
with automatic rifle AK-47 ('Kalashnikov')
in summer Battle Dress.

Motorized troops
with a light machine-gun RPD (Degtjarew)
in winter Battle Dress.

Service Rank Insignia

Private

Lance-corporal

Sergeant
CSM

Battalion-Sergeant

Sergeant-major

2nd Lieutenant

Captain

Colonel

Colonel-general

Chief Marshal

Armoured Corps Private

Paratrooper

Marine-Infantryman

Aircraft Pilot

Insignia

Airborne Troops

Air force

Armoured Corps

Technical Section of the Air force

Cockade (officers)

Motorized Rifle Troops

Technical Section of the Army

Aircraft Insignia

Traffic Control

Cockade (NCOs and men)

Army Service Corps (Transport)

Medical

Signals

Artillery

Traffic controller's helmet

Field Cap

Guards' Badge

The badges denoting arm of service are worn on the collar patches.

Corporal with AK-47 in summer Battle Dress (linen uniform)

Motorized trooper with AK-47 in winter Battle Dress (cloth uniform)

Motorized trooper in winter Battle Dress with Greatcoat and Field Cap

Sub-Lieutenant in winter Battle Dress with overcoat and Field Cap

Service rank insignia

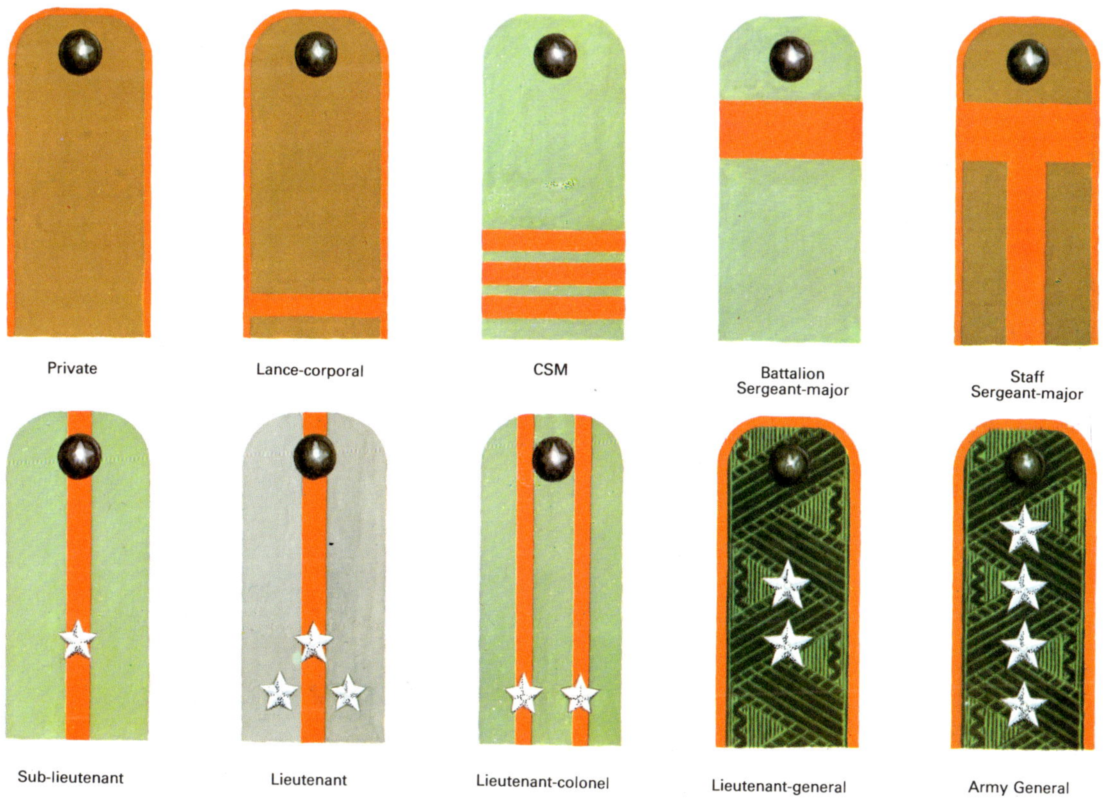

With all four kinds of uniform, the steel helmet, Field Cap or Fur Cap may be worn. The colour of the shoulder straps bearing the badge of rank indicates the different kind of uniform.

2nd Lieutenant
of Motorized Troops
in summer Battle Dress

Camouflage dress
worn by Paratroops
and Border Troops

Mountain soldier
with AK-47 machine-carbine
in winter equipment

Armoured trooper
in winter equipment

Badges

Transport trooper

Signals trooper

Service Corps
trooper

Motorized trooper

Officer's
winter Fur Cap

Administration

Medical

Cockade

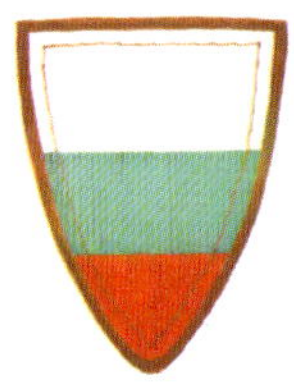

Nationality badge

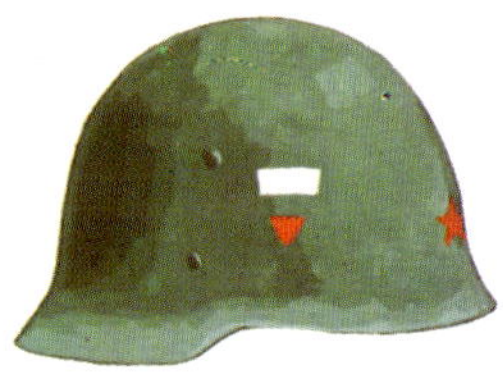

Steel helmet

Engineers

Armoured Corps

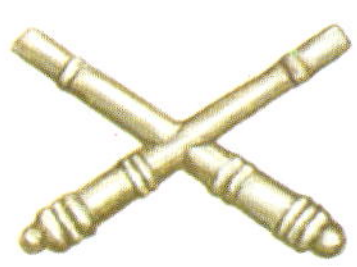

Artillery

Airborne

Officer's cap badge
(cockade)

Collar Tabs
for motorized troops
for Generals

Nationality badges are worn on the steel helmet and Field Cap. Collar Tabs are worn on Greatcoats and winter Battle Dress (cloth).

Motorized Troops
with AK-47 machine-carbines
in summer Battle Dress
in winter Battle Dress

Sub-Lieutenant
of the Motorized Troops
in summer Battle Dress

Member of the
'Workers Combat Teams'

Badges

Private

Regimental lance-corporal

NCO (corporal)

CSM

Battalion Sergeant-major

Staff Sergeant-major

Cap badge (cockade)

Sub-lieutenant

Captain

Lieutenant-colonel

Major-general

Army General

Arm badge of a 'Workers Combat Team'

There is no Battle Dress for Generals. On active service they wear Service Dress with appropriate badges of rank.

Motorized trooper in Battle Dress

Corporal in light winter Battle Dress

Major in summer Battle Dress

Private — NCO — CSM — Battalion Sergeant-major — Sergeant-major — Chief Staff Sergeant-major — Ensign

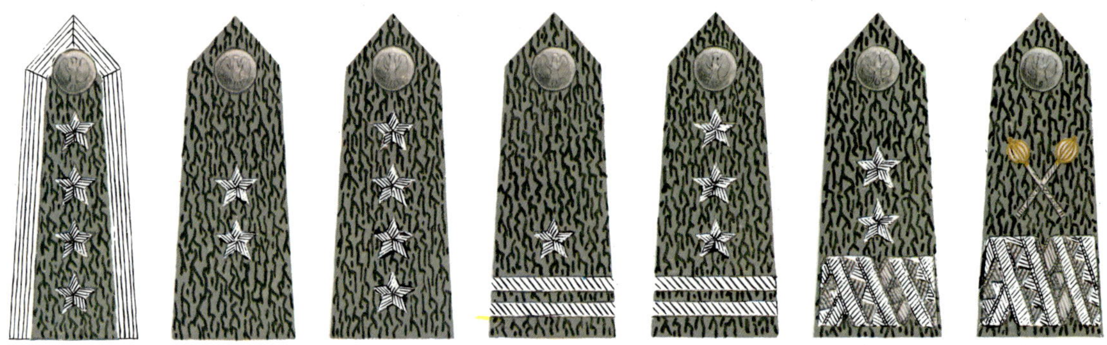

Chief Ensign — 2nd Lieutenant — Captain — Major — Lieutenant-colonel — Divisional General — Marshal of Poland

Armoured Corps trooper

Paratrooper in summer Battle Dress

Staff Sergeant-major in summer Battle Dress (Marine-Infantry)

Ensign in the Air Force in Service Dress

Cap Badges

Army

Army

Navy

Air force

Infantry

Artillery

Armoured Corps

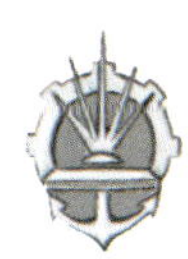
Marine-Infantry

Medical

Aircrew

Wireless operator

Supplies

Engineers

Military Police

Military Police

Motorized troop with AK-47 machine-carbine in summer Battle Dress

Corporal with AK-47 in winter Battle Dress

Soldier of the Border Troops with AK-47 in Battle Dress

Service Rank Insignia

Private (Railway Corps)

Corporal (Motorized)

Sergeant (Armoured Corps)

Battalion Sergeant-major (Artillery)

Staff Sergeant-major (Airborne)

Military Master 4th Class (Border Troop)

Military Master 1st Class (Signals)

Reserve Sub-Lieutenant (Border Troops)

Lieutenant (Administration)

Captain (Armoured Corps)

Major (Technical Service) Field Dress

Colonel (Airborne)

Lieutenant-general

Army General

Field Uniforms have rank insignia of the same colour as the uniform material, as illustrated above in the case of the Major (Technical Service). These, however, are seldom worn.

In practice, one sees, almost invariably, the coloured Service Rank Insignia belonging to Service and Walking Out Dress on the Field Uniform.

Sergeant of Mountain Troops

Armoured Corps captain

Helicopter pilot

Member of the 'Patriotic Guard'

Badges

Motorized troops

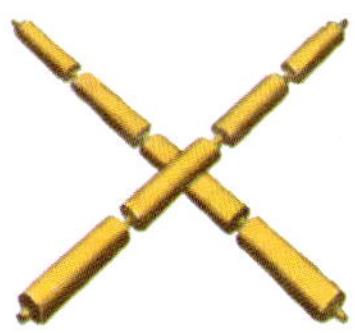

Artillery

Officers' cap badge

Other ranks' cap badge

Signals

Border Troops

Airborne

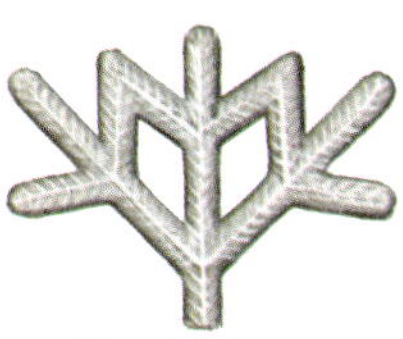

Mountain troops

Medical Corps

Armoured Corps

Helmet of Traffic Controllers

Field Cap

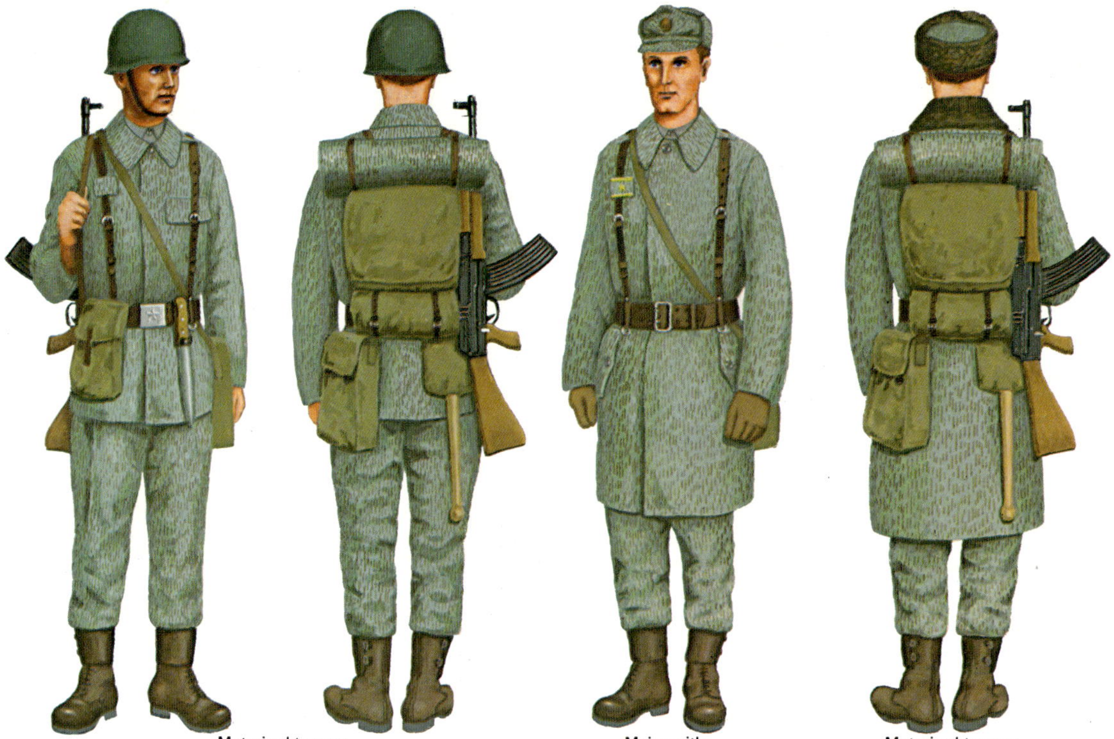

Motorized trooper with AK-47 automatic rifle ('Kalashnikov') in summer Battle Dress

Major with Field Cap and Greatcoat

Motorized trooper in winter Battle Dress

Service Rank Insignia

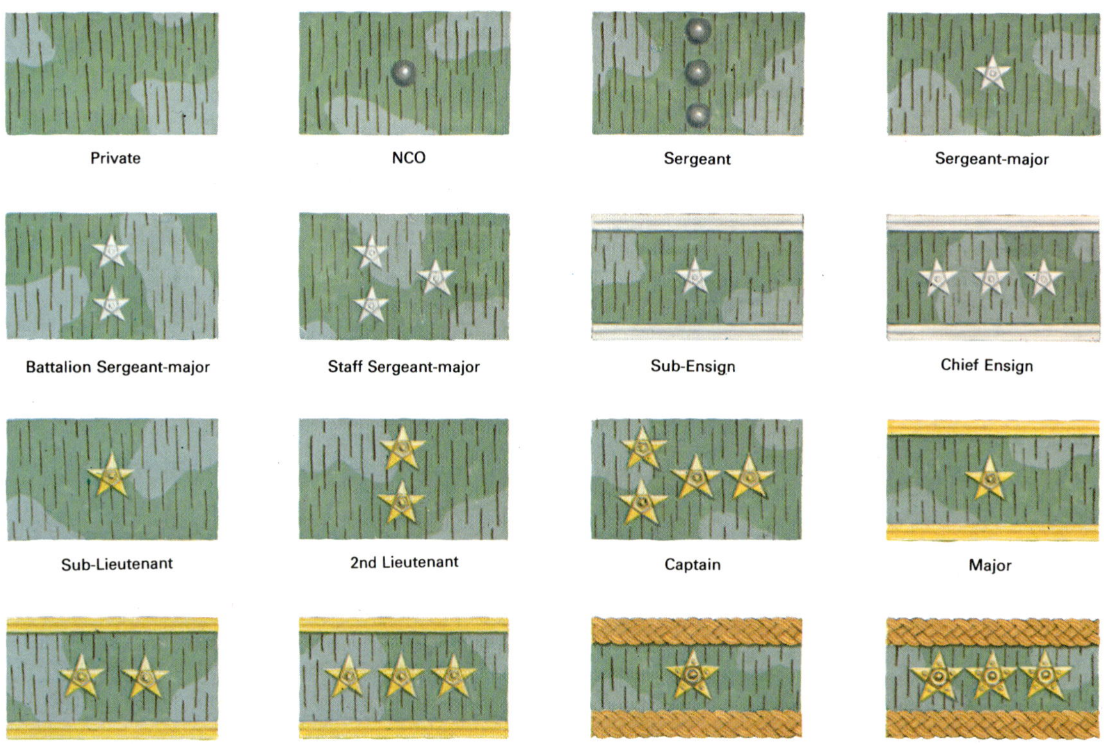

Private

NCO

Sergeant

Sergeant-major

Battalion Sergeant-major

Staff Sergeant-major

Sub-Ensign

Chief Ensign

Sub-Lieutenant

2nd Lieutenant

Captain

Major

Lieutenant-colonel

Colonel

Major-general

Colonel-general

On the Battle Dress, service rank insignia is worn on the right breast.

Protective uniform for tank crews

Paratrooper's Battle Dress

2nd Lieutenant with Fur Cap and winter Greatcoat

People's Militiaman

Cap insignia

Airborne troops' arm badge

Traffic Controllers' helmet

Service Branch Badges

Infantry

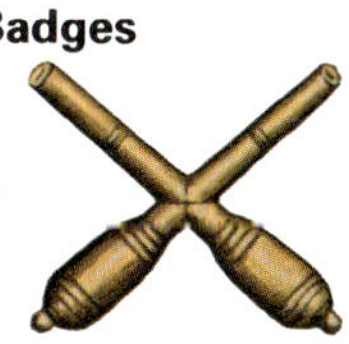

Artillery

Anti-aircraft

Armoured Corps

Air force

Airborne Troops

Engineers

Nuclear/ Chemical Defence

Railway Corps

Medical Corps

Supply Corps

Border Guards

Service badges are not worn on the Battle Dress. They are displayed only on the collar patches of the Service and Walking Out uniforms.

Motorized infantryman with AK-47 machine-carbine ('Kalashnikov') in summer Battle Dress

Motorized infantryman with AK-47 in transitional uniform with Field Cap / winter Battle Dress with Fur Cap.

Service Rank Insignia

Private · Lance-corporal · Corporal (NCO) · Platoon Commander (Sergeant) · CSM · Staff Sergeant-major · Chief Ensign

Sub-Lieutenant · 2nd Lieutenant · Captain · Major · Colonel · Major-general · Colonel-general

Service rank insignia are worn on both shoulder straps and on the left side of the Field Cap.

Lieutenant
in summer Battle Dress

Armoured Corps trooper
in winter equipment

Traffic Control Corps trooper
in winter Battle Dress

Member of the
Workers
Militia

Service Branch Badges

Motorized troops

Anti-tank Corps

Airborne Troop

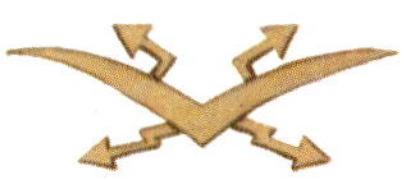

Signals of Air force

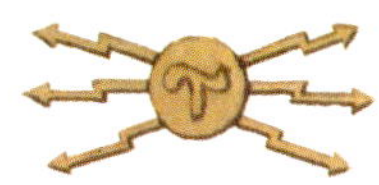

Signals of Army

Medical
Corps

Technical
Corps

Armoured Corps

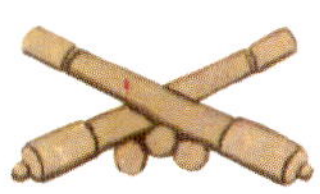

Artillery

Service
Corps

Repair/
Mechanical Corps

Supply troops

Helmet of Traffic Control Corps
('F' = Formgalomszabályazás)

Cap badge
(cockade)

Field Cap
(corporal)

Service branch badges are not worn on Battle Dress; they are shown only on the collar patches of Service and Walking Out dress.

Private
with M-56 submachine-gun
in summer Battle Dress

Private
with M-48 carbine
in winter Battle Dress

Tank Corps private

Mountain trooper
in winter equipment

Service Rank Insignia

Corporal · Sergeant-major · Squadron Sergeant-major · Staff Sergeant-major · CSM · Ensign · 1st Ensign

Sub-Lieutenant · Captain · Captain (1st Class) · Major · Lieutenant-colonel · Major-general · Army General

Soviet Union

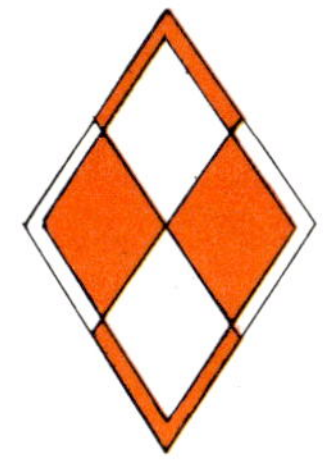
Poland

National Insignia for Vehicles

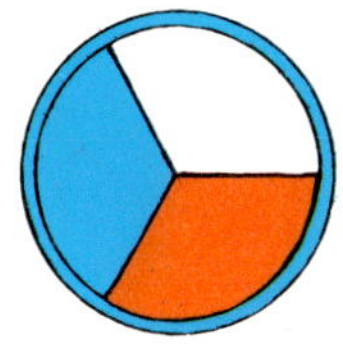
Czechoslovakia

German Democratic Republic

Hungary

Bulgaria

Romania

Poland

Airborne Insignia

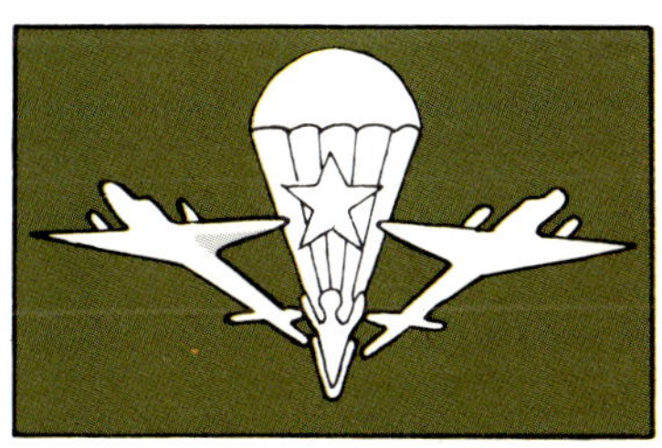
Soviet Union

Czechoslovakia

National Insignia for Aircraft

Soviet Union

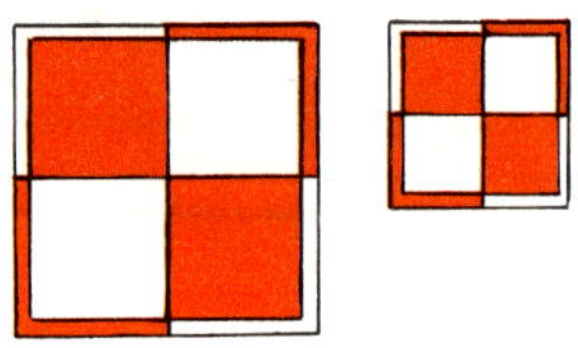

Poland

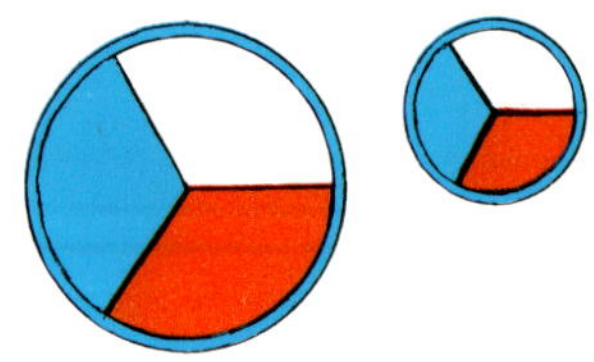

Czechoslovakia

German Democratic Republic

Hungary

Romania

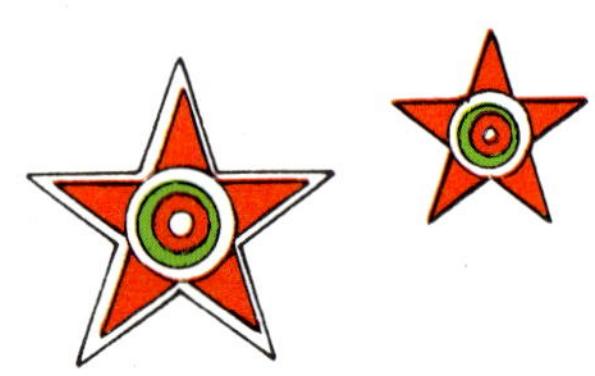

Bulgaria

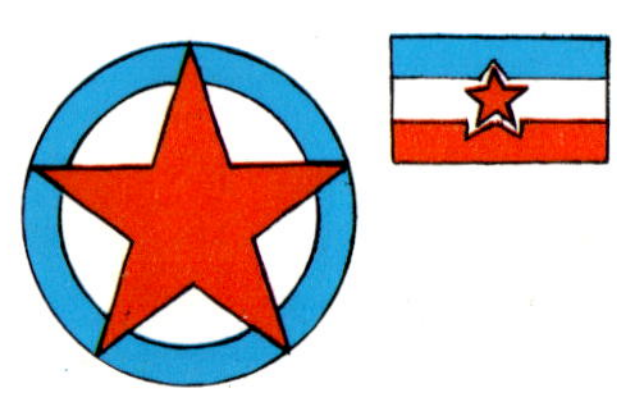

Yugoslavia